THE TRUE

DEFINITION OF

FREEDOM

Marvin Dearing

ISBN-13: 978-0692293294 (Midnight Express Books)

ISBN-10: 0692293299

Logo designed by Kevin Kimbrough

Published by

Midnight Express Books

POBox 69
Berryville, AR 72616
http://www.MidnightExpressBooks.com

ACKNOWLEDGMENTS

I would like to thank my mother, Mrs. Earlene Dearing who has supported me through my many struggles. Much love always.

My daughters, Rosa and Diamond, who are my inspiration.

And the Gods who have showed me the true path to eternal life.

Victor and Linda Huddleston who kept me posted in every process; your integrity is impeccable!

To Gary Roberts A.K.A. G-rilla; stay up and keep building.

To Bommani Shakur and the Lucasville Five - stay up!

To my artist Kevin Kimbrough, A.K.A. Mix Tape, you're a born artist.

To humanity of all colors and classes – God loves.

To Detroit Zilla, you're next. Keep writing! You're a natural poet.

ACKNOWLEDGEMENT

Contents

INTRODUCTION

In today's society most people are unhappy, confused, and distracted. Our modern culture has placed way too much energy in developing fashion trends, violence, excessive sexual content due to heavy media exposure from radio and television. As a result, we as the human race have become out of touch with our natural selves. If we are to save society and its people from destruction then a blueprint of self-empowerment and spiritual oneness must be laid out and followed, it is from all my trials and tribulations and the sake of lost humanity that has inspired me to write this book. As Colin Powell, the former Secretary of State of the United States of America stated: *"None of us can change our yesterdays but all of us can change our tomorrows"*. Freedom is often defined as being free to choose between poverty, wealth, sexual preference, or physical incarceration. While it is essential for you to exercise those types of freedom if you choose, however, those types of freedom doesn't determine our happiness, self-esteem nor spiritual cultivation. How many times have you seen or heard about a famous actress; singer, or hard worker with material wealth committing suicide? Or engaging in excessive drug or alcohol abuse? We all probably know or heard of a few. Once a balance between the material and spiritual is attained we will come into the real realization of ourselves and experience true happiness, internal peace, and soundness of mind. You will begin to set all your judgments and criticism aside and realize all humanity is one. This new knowledge will allow you to appreciate and recognize yourself as a special unique individual with many talents and capabilities. Your eyes will be open to new realities.

In December of 1998 a string of events took place in my life that was so severe that my life was changed completely. I felt I was being cursed by God. I was unhappy with life and myself. To compensate for my lack of happiness, I became a heavy consumer of marijuana and liquor. My self-esteem was so low I could barely get out of bed at times. My family noticed the strange behavior I was displaying. I wasn't living up to their expectations of me. I rarely went to visit my daughter for fear of her seeing me in that negative condition. 1 was embarrassed and considered myself a looser. In my mind, the world owed me something and my anger at society was justified. The excessive use of marijuana only helped to create more confusion. In my mind, I wasted to escape but realistically I became my own worst enemy running from myself. I felt as if I was trapped inside a hellish cycle and couldn't get out. On December 23rd I went to a friend's house to get high and drunk which was the usual for me, I left the party around 12:30am. My cousin's house was my destination. She would have been happy to see me and when I finally arrived she was shocked and scared as if she was looking at a ghost. Just before I made it to her house I was approached by a tall man with a gun in his hand. Many things were going through my mind. Questions like, "What is this?", "Is this a joke?", were hounding me. Something of my intuition warned me that this scene was real. The gunman was demanding money from me. I was being robbed by this stranger. Before I can reach in my pocket and give him the $50.00 cash I had, I heard an explosion, Pop, my mouth began to feel abnormally wet. Blood was oozing all over me. It was then I realized I had been shot. The gunman turned around and ran. I started running towards my cousin's house. Luckily there was a hospital located around the corner from where she lived. The bullet caught me in the upper lip, knocked out one of my side teeth and lodged in my neck. The doctors said it was a miracle I survived such a fatal shooting without my face being heavily disfigured. After that incident something else happened to me that I will never forget. On February 19 1999, I received a strange vision. A very familiar face surrounded by a bright light appeared to me. A deep voice then called my name and told me that I am being chosen to partake in the uplifting of humanity. I reached out with my right hand and tried to touch the face which then disappeared. After the vision I began to feel very different. The feeling was that I had been newly born. A fresh wave of energy had embraced me. The craving to smoke pot and get drunk was somehow removed from me. I began attending school at Tri Community College. My family was proud that I had finally stopped partying so much and decided to get my life together. Unfortunately, life had more trials and tribulations awaiting me. On January 3rd 2000 I was arrested and charged with murder. On July 19th I was tried and convicted and sentenced to 18-to-life in a maximum security prison. I couldn't understand why this was happening to me after I began to turn my life around. Everyone knew I was innocent. I later discovered that the prosecutor withheld information that could have set me free. I asked God why he was allowing the judicial system to convict an innocent man. It seemed as if God wasn't concerned with my questions. Something was in my way to destroy my life. Someone or something had put a curse on me and I warned to know who was behind this bad luck I was having. I felt like giving up. It was then that I thought I saw that night in a vision I was reminded that I was fighting a war on a spiritual plane. Even though I had been done wrong by a system who incarcerates innocent people, prison does not dictate my action nor does it determine my self-worth. The journey of life works in mysterious ways. If I have to suffer incarceration for humanity to receive this message, my will will not be broken. The government of the ancient Romans persecuted Jesus when he came to deliver prophecies to the people of his time. Let's begin our journey into the book.

CHAPTER 1 – Mind Over Matter

Most people have a tendency to overlook or undervalue the power of the mind. When the average person thinks of the mind they imagine this huge, gigantic brain inside our head that's connected to our shoulders. While this may be true to an extent, however, a stronger analysis will give us a deeper understanding of the mind and its powers. The mind is where we construct our thoughts and wishes. Thoughts are very important in our life because they are what determine the quality of our life and the way we see ourselves. For example: Take two people who grew up in the worst poverty conditions. One rose above his conditions of poverty and the other allowed his impoverished environment to take him under. The reason the former man succeeded was because despite his environmental conditions he was always engaged in positive thoughts that he would one day rise to success and provide a better life for him and his family. The latter individual didn't succeed because most of his thoughts were negative. He spent most of his time complaining about his conditions and feeling sorry for himself instead of him being inspired to achieve better life conditions. He became overly pessimistic and blaming others for his problems. Consequently he became a failure. Your mind can be a guide to prosperity or it can be your worst enemy. Thought are actions in the form of mental images. The universal laws of magnetic gravity shows and proves that when the mind begins to think a thought, the mental energy begins to attract the desired objective. The thought will seek conscious expression and must materialize whether the thought is good or bad. We must always be aware of the thoughts we are thinking. In some instances, our thoughts become distorted from past negative events. Most people have unfinished business from their childhood. Some people were abused by their parents mentally or physically or they feel their parents weren't there for them enough. For the most part, our physiological problems almost always stem from how we interacted with our parents and peers. In our early age if the experience was negative, we may grow up with resentment, anger, and low self-esteem. The frustration will sometimes carry into our social dealings or personal relationships with our spouse. When this type of dynamic occurs, your mind will begin to turn on itself. Your spouse may be the right person to be in a relationship with, but because your mind is clogged up with negative emotions such as fear, anger, low self-esteem, it's hard for you to see the beauty and potential in the other person because you are unaware of the good qualities in yourself. You end up destroying what could have been a wonderful opportunity to experience a long lasting healthy relationship. Fears and insecurities come from a lack of knowing who we are and what our purpose in life is. We usually end up conforming to a fixed ideal that's not our own. Hoping it will work for us and believing that's who we are. We simply want to become someone else.

All our ideals come from other people telling us who we are or what we should be doing even if it's not right for us. Consequently most people seek approval from others without approving of themselves. When we dwell on our negative experiences we are attracting for ourselves a cycle of those same type of negative events. It is hard for us to forget the bad things we have suffered in life. However, when we view those experiences in an optimistic manner we develop a positive thought pattern which enables us to grow positively from the experience. The mind is the main foundation of our existences. Without it the body could not function. Here's a perfect analogy to describe the relationship between the mind and the body. It's similar to an automobile. The mind is the engine while the body is the vehicle. The body could be beautiful on the outside. However, the body would not be able to operate without the engine. The radio and windshield wipers would not work. Along with using the engine to keep the body working is making sure the engine is fed a good quality of oil. A periodic tune up is essential for keeping the engine lasting longer and running smoothly. We must feed our minds with a good quality of education and good thoughts. If you tell yourself you won't succeed then you will attract for yourself all the necessary tools of failure. If you visualize yourself achieving your goals every day, you will gain energy and attract the people and things needed to help you reach your goals. Visualization is a powerful tool. I will go into more detail in the next chapter. Negative thoughts will send signals to the body that will cause the body to weaken and eventually sicken. Stress is the number one killer in our society. Let our journey continue.

CHAPTER 2 – The Power Within

Before the planets, earth and humans were born only two types of energy existed, (1) Potential energy and (2) Kinetic energy. Potential energy is energy that is dormant, immovable, or formless. While kinetic energy is energy in motion. Once a thought to create is formed potential energy becomes kinetic energy attracting matter to produce creation on a material level. This is possible through the magnetic laws of gravity. Out of this magnetic motion our universe, planets, animals, and humans were born. Humans are a very unique species. What makes humans more prominent then those animals in the lower animal kingdom is the human's ability to reason. Whereas on the contrary animals from the lower ranks are born with a programmed instinct that limits their brain capacity. Humans can use their brain to create whatever it is they wish. Civilizations, modern civilizations built automobiles figured out the rotation of planets, crested cures for the sick, etc. As the great Bible stated: 'God made man in his own likeness,' Chapter one verse 27 (Bible). Being made in the likeness of God means we all have the potential to become Godlike. When humans dwelled in the Garden of Eden they knew of no bad luck or strife. They were in total bliss, hi feet the Garden of Eden is symbolic to a state of calmness and peace in an environment minus evil. The first people Adam and Eve tell from the Garden of Eden when Eve and Adam ate off the tree of knowledge. Consequently they were removed from the Garden of Eden. That event is symbolic to the fall of man. As a result humans became aware of evil and intoned to negative vices such as hatred, greed, envy, jealousy, and all types of evil elements. Those evil vices became desirable to humans. It was written and recorded by 24 ancient wise deters that in order for humans to return back to that blissful state or Garden of Eden they would have to undergo a process of evolution. They would have to experience life at polarities of good and evil. This balance would be consistent in giving the human race motivation to destroy the negative vices within them and build on their righteous qualities. Only then will man return back into his natural essence which is peace, calmness of that Garden of Eden. This process of self-gratification is done by first acknowledging your negative ways and actions. Tell yourself that you want to be a better person; once this is done you have made the first step to success. Remember that is only the first step life will still deliver its test and challenges. The next step you should take some time alone to analyze yourself. Start from the days from when you were a child up until your present time. If you can't remember your childhood days don't worry. Just do the best you can to remember any events that were relevant in your life. Analyze your actions and deeds, even your frustrations and the times that make you happy. This self reflection will cause you to become familiar with your strengths and weaknesses. Proper meditation will also help you achieve this state. So many books have been written on meditation I can't count them all but there is only one proper way to meditate. Proper meditation is done by first exercising proper breathing techniques. When you understand bow important proper breathing is you will begin to exercise these tactics and feel better. We extend our life when we breathe correctly. Our life pulse is stronger. Our heartbeat slows down to eliminate a lot of anxiety. We amply develop more energy as we return back into our natural state of calmness and peacefulness. No worries or frustrations. To begin when you're alone lay on your back with your hands on your side. Relax every part of your body. Erase every thought from your mind with your eyes closed. Take a deep breath: inhale. At the stage that you are inhaling your stomach should be pushed out while you are inhaling. Now hold it and count to eight. Now exhale. At the stage of your exhale your stomach should be pushed in. Repeat the exercise until your body reaches full relaxation. Sometimes your body will feel like its floating or you may feel flashes of heat, that's normal, indicating that you have reached your natural state. Now you are prepared to exercise the creative visualization process. Begin to paint a mental picture of you obtaining your wishes. If could be anything that you wish for; it doesn't matter. Allow your thoughts to come to you naturally. It's just like watching television in your head with your brain being the screen and your thoughts being the remote control. You are tuning into whatever thoughts that you wish. Thoughts eventually become actions. Your physical being will move to materialize whatever it is that you visualize. There is a natural law of the universe that we attract the things that we think about the most. The meditation process will maximize your visualizes calming your mind so uncontrollable thoughts won't enter your mind while you're trying to visualize your thoughts. Whenever you find yourself overwhelmed by stress of any kind use the breathing techniques. This will help you see things more clear. Your mind will become more focused. When we make decisions while were angry we usually end up making bad chokes. Anger clouds our ability to make clear productive choices that will have a positive effect on our life. A lot of times we spend too much time day dreaming a happy ending. We want to believe that everything will be alright without us taking the necessary action to obtain what we want Then when we are faced with some unexpected change of fortune we become very disappointed about the outcome. When the truth is: "Life is full of ups and downs, twist and turns. The key is not to expect life to always deliver us a box of roses but the goal is to build up enough strength to be able to ride the wave of life to the finish line." Endurance and perseverance should be our aim. We have to see ourselves doing better but the most important part is to take some action as to what we are trying to achieve. We have the power to become whatever we wish. We were created in the image of God. Low self-esteem and stress are nothing but self-imposed weaknesses tint hold us back. Don't become your own enemy. Think highly of yourself and others will regard you in high esteem. Decide for yourself what it is that you want in life. Then begin to move in the direction of your goals. Visualizing what you want will naturally attract for you the proper people and opportunities that will help you reach your destination. Good dieting and adequate exercise will strengthen your mind and spirit.

Marvin Dearing

CHAPTER 3 – You Are What You Eat

Food is what we use for nourishment of the body. It is what gives us the energy we need to carry out our worldly task. However, certain foods such as red meats and excessive sugar foods can have a detrimental effect on our health. We usually develop a sluggish feeling along with physical problems like colon cancer, heart diseases, high blood pressure and for most people an early death is the end result. When the animals are slaughtered meat producers have already injected the animals with chemicals such as steroids for the purpose of fatting up the animals. The slaughtered animals are then shipped from the meat producer to the local grocery stores where it is sold to meat consumers. The meats sit on our stomach for days before it is finally digested. In the meantime the meat is spoiling and rotten inside us. That's why when we defecate it smells real badly. The rotten meat also attracts a lot of bacteria that causes us sickness. We would live along time if we wouldn't eat red meat. Not only would we be healthier but we would have more energy. You would also begin to look younger. A person who eats healthy on a regular basis could be 60 years old but look 30. I get compliments on how I look all the time. People always tell me I look younger than 35. Eating a lot of fried foods also has the same negative effect on the body. The grease will clog main arteries causing heart attacks frequently. Although most Americans don't like to eat vegetables however, fresh vegetables are good for us. Vegetables like carrots, beans, and spinach are rich in vitamins and calcium. They are also good for our skin and heart. Instead of pigging out on a lot of sweets for a snack eat some fresh fruit. Eating a lot of sweets will de-energize you as well as cause you to become overweight. Excessive amounts of sugar and salt are dangerous to your health. Your body is your temple for your mind and soul. We should always strive to feed it proper nutrients. Adequate exercise is essential for good bodily health. Every morning before you begin your daily routine get some good exercising in. Exercising will send oxygen to the right side of your brain helping your brain become more functional. That's why when we exercise we get that rush like a light headed feeling. Physical exercising will heighten your thinking process. It's very important that we take good care of our physical health. What's the good of being materially successful if our body isn't in good health? We would be weighed down by all kinds of physical sicknesses. In the ancient days when the human race was living more intoned with nature biblical prophets lived in the physical flesh for hundreds of years. In modem society where the air is polluted from so much carbon dioxide we are exposed to greater contamination. The animals too are at risk of these same types of germs and bacteria. The life span for the average American is 75 years. However, if we take care of our health by eating the right foods and exercising regularly we would prolong our life. Positive thinking will also decrease depression.

Some people overeat due to depression and stress which causes the body to weaken and deteriorate; you cannot cure problems of fear and anxiety by overeating. It will only make the problems worse. Practice the visualization and meditation techniques to combat stress and you will grow much stronger physically and spiritually.

Marvin Dearing

CHAPTER 4 – Turn A Negative Experience Into A Positive Experience

Trials and tribulations are part of the evolving process for human beings. A lot of times we tend to overreact to the trials and tests we go through. Negative experiences too often leaves people exhausted, fatigued, and unable to bounce back. When we allow the bad times to make us feel anger that will cause depression, we fail to see the positive message in die experience. Life on this planet Earth can be imagined as a training school. The trouble we sometimes face, the people we meet are all there to help us graduate to the next level or higher existence. I can remember a time when I was 16 years old I had a summer job as a construction worker. We were reconstructing an old high school building. The building hadn't been occupied in about five years. I was happy to have the job. I was saving money to purchase my first car. I had to be at work at 7:00am to 4:00pm for four days a week. Sometimes we would work late into the evening. One morning I was so in a rush to get to work that I was running late. It was Monday and I was out partying with friends that whole weekend so I had unintentionally over slept. On my way to the bus stop I ran into a kid I knew who was 17 with no job but always drives different cars. I asked him if he could drive me to work When he was glad to assist me I was happy I wouldn't have to take the bus. It wasn't no longer than 15 minutes after I was in the car than the police got behind us flashing their sirens indicating for us to pull the car over. My driving buddy decided he didn't want to stop for anybody especially the police. All I wanted was a lair ride to work and here I was on a high speed chase down Kinsman Avenue trying to talk to my friend was useless. He was determined he wasn't going to stop. Next thing I remember we were crashing dead smack into a pole. The police were at our windows with their guns out. We were roughly pulled out of the car, handcuffed and thrown into the police car. That's when I discovered the car was really stolen. We were rushed to the detention center where I spent 72 hours before my mom was able to come and spring me out. My mom was so angry when she found out what happened. I thought I was going to die. Mom gave me the lecture all the way home and for the next two weeks. Although the experience was kind of rough I had learned a valuable lesson. I should have just simply took the bus to work and explained the truth to my boss and hoped he would have some understanding. I have never made being late for work a priority. I also learned that when you rush things you will sometimes create more problems in the process that will require you to spend more time fixing so you still end up late anyway. Life is always testing us with unexpected challenges we all want more of the rosy side of life. The problem with this type of thought process is we often are left unprepared to deal with the sudden twist and turns of life. When we face reality that things don't always go as planned we better equip ourselves to deal with whatever awaits us. Knowledge, wisdom, and understanding are three of the most precious tools ever. You will make decisions not based on material passions, lust, love or need but you will learn to make decisions based on the law of the truth. Whether it makes you feel good or not simply stand up to them. Tell them "No you don't want to get high" "You have to study for class " Or "No I don't want to steal this car with you " They can't force you to partake in the destruction of your dreams. You are in control of your own life. You lead your own destination. Be wise and patient. Work hard to achieve success any failures will supply give you with the wisdom to begin again. You will eventually succeed.

Marvin Dearing

CHAPTER 5 – Good Company or Bad Company

As human beings we are very empathic people. We become like the people we most spend our time with. If we surround ourselves with negative people all day that negative energy will rub off on us. Just like if we surround ourselves with successful people we will become inspired to want to achieve like them. Human beings are walking energy volts. They let off magnetic waves of energy according to their personality or even feelings that they feel at a specific moment these waves of energy also has the ability to attract other energy. These energetic forces have a scientific power of their own. For example: have you ever been in a room and another person walked in and you suddenly felt it was something about that person negative or positive? You probably didn't know it but you were feeling the other person's energy. Most people feel the feeling but actually pay no attention to it. Say if it was a negative feeling you felt about someone but you still went ahead and decided the person was alright so you accepted the friendship. Then later on down the road the person turned out to be very negative. Then you say to yourself; "Dam I should have followed my first mind I knew it was something about that person." Too often we choose friends out of loneliness or a need to be accepted. Once you come to realize that you weren't a mistake on the planet. You will begin to feel your sense of worth. You won't need other people to validate yourself worth. Each and every human on this planet has something special and unique about them. It could be your ability to bring cheer to a suffering person. Your talent in the arts, music, labor, poetry perhaps you have suffered tremendous difficulties in your life. You will become extremely wise in the aftermath considering you have a positive outlook. Whatever the case we all have a purpose on this planet. The people we associate with are very critical. People who are always gossiping negatively about others will only drain your energy. Those types of folks say they create negative sessions that tears down. They speak words of insult and divisions. Next time you find yourself in the company of these types of individuals do not allow yourself to become attached or influenced by their thinking. Their problems are deep rooted and psychological. They have given up on their dreams. They have become bitter and angry at their selves and the world. Once they see potential in you they will quickly move to discourage you. They will say things like "You're not good enough," or "You will probably fail," or "You're not rich enough to get started." Positive people speak words that uplift and create positive energy. If you don't have a keen sense of self worth you will allow yourself to get caught up by someone else's negative thinking. You will leave a conversation with them feeling depressed and unhappy. The world is full of individuals who have failed to cultivate their potential to the fullest due to wanting to please another person who does not have their best interest at heart. These people probably had a lot to offer the world but they allowed the peer pressure from negative people to destroy their potential. Positive people are the ones who will encourage you to follow your dreams.

They will say things like; "Nothing is impossible," "I believe you can do it," or "You can be anything you want to be." Next time you are confronted by negative people who wish to steer your course away from your goals. Next time you are confronted by negativity don't panic or get angry. Relax and ask yourself what the experience is trying to show you. Take a more objective approach and you will always find wisdom within the situation whatever it is.

Marvin Dearing

ABOUT THE AUTHOR

The author, Marvin Dearing, is currently incarcerated in Ohio due to wrongful conviction. However, Dearing has earned a Doctor's degree of Divinity and is an ordained minister who has helped hundreds of people in Ohio find their true inner self.

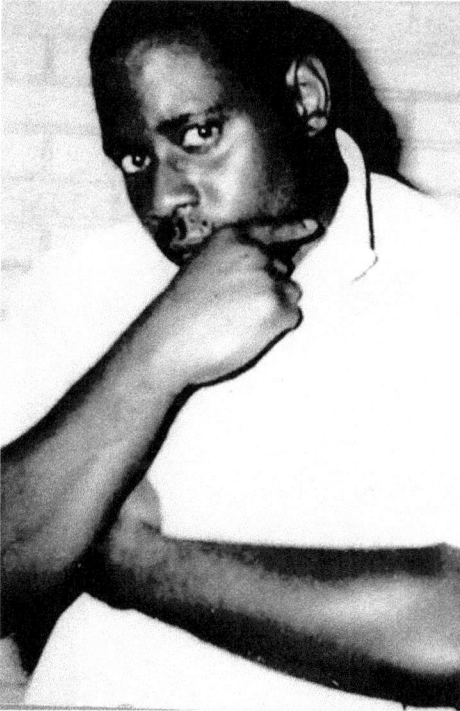

Dearing is also the founder and organizer of S.O.U.L. School of Universal Light which provides lessons and support to those seeking spiritual cultivation.

Contact the author at:

Marvin Dearing

#421-030
POBox 45699
Lucasville, Ohio 45699
Email:
marvindearing@yahoo.com

Marvin Dearing

www.ingramcontent.com/pod-product-compliance
Lightning Source LLC
Chambersburg PA
CBHW060547030426
42337CB00021B/4478